I feel bullied

Written by Jen Green

Illustrated by Mike Gordon

HODDER
Wayland

an imprint of Hodder Children's Books

When I feel bullied I feel hurt,
I feel frightened, I feel small ...

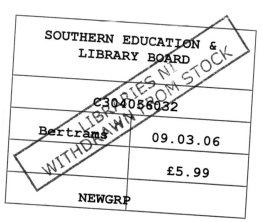

Then I tell my mum and dad,
and now I feel tall.

When I feel bullied ...

my tummy ties
itself in knots ...

I find it hard to
sleep at night ...

I feel all alone,
with no-one to
talk to …

I find it hard to eat.

7

When a big boy chases after me and pulls my hair, I feel bullied.

But I say 'OW!' loudly, so everyone knows what is going on.

When the girls
make fun of my
new spectacles
and call me names,
I feel bullied.

But the teacher notices, and
tells the girls to stop.

When my sister takes my toys and breaks them, I feel bullied.

But she is only cross because our big brother has been bullying her.

13

When the gang makes fun of my friend and his family, he feels bullied.

But he comes and plays
with me instead.

Some grown-ups say, 'hit the bully back'.

Hit the bully back!

But hitting back can make things a lot worse.

17

Grown-ups can feel bullied too ...

... and grown-ups can be bullies.

19

If I feel bullied, it helps to think about nice things, or something I am good at.

When I pretend I don't care, the bully gives up and goes away.

Sometimes I feel brave enough to stand up for myself.

I tell the bully to stop it,
then I walk away.

Leave
me alone!

If I feel bullied, often the best thing to do is to tell a grown-up.

It might be Mum or Dad, my teacher or a dinner lady.

My teacher says no one should bully anyone.

Bullies need to talk. They often feel unhappy too.

27

If I see someone being bullied, I don't just stand by and let it happen.

If we can't stop the bullying,
we tell a grown-up who
will sort it out.

Notes for parents and teachers

This book provides an introduction to the subject of bullying for young children. Parents or teachers who have read the book with children, either individually or in groups, may find it useful to stop and discuss issues as they come up.

Encourage children to talk about situations in which they felt bullied. Which of the ideas on pages 4-7 are closest to how children feel and react to being bullied? Can they illustrate how they feel?

Bullying can involve physical violence, taking someone's money or possessions, name-calling and teasing, or just leaving someone out. Children might like to write short poems about real or imaginary situations, addressed to the bully and repeating the phrase 'I feel bullied':

When you make fun of me and call me names, I feel bullied.

When you push me in the playground, I feel bullied.

This book shows various ways of dealing with bullying. Sometimes it is possible for children to stand up to a bully. At other times it is best to to ignore the situation, or to walk away.

Children might like to explore various situations, and discuss the best way of dealing with each. Encourage children to act out saying no to a bully. Other children can comment on whether the scene acted out was realistic. How else might the situation have been resolved?

Explain that in many situations, it is best to tell an adult about bullying. Stress that this is not telling tales, it is often the bravest thing to do. Explain that a grown-up can often sort out the situation without the bully knowing anyone has told. Emphasize that bullying is always wrong, and should be stopped as quickly as possible.

The book suggests various reasons why children bully others. Encourage the children to talk about whether they have ever bullied, or felt like bullying someone. Children may start bullying because they feel unhappy, jealous, or lonely. Others want to look tough, be part of a gang, or are being bullied themselves.

If children see others being bullied, they may feel scared to speak up in case they are picked on next. Remind them what it feels like to be bullied. The class may decide that bullying is not allowed, and that everyone will help if they see someone being bullied.

Use this book for teaching literacy

This book can help you in the literacy hour in the following ways:

- ✓ Children can write simple stories linked to personal experience using the language of the text in this book as a model for their own writing. (Year 1, Term 3: Non-fiction writing composition)

- ✓ Use of speech bubbles and enlarged print shows different ways of presenting texts. (Year 2, Term 2: Sentence construction and punctuation)

Books to read

Bully written by Janine Amos, illustrated by Gwen Green (Cherrytree Press, 2001). Michael, Sharon and Li are all bullies. With the help of Michael's friend James, Sharon's teacher and Li's mum, they talk about their feelings and realise that the bullying has to stop.

Rosie and the Pavement Bears by Susie Jenkin-Pearce (Red Fox Picture Books, 1992). Rosie is the smallest girl in her class. The class bullies, Ben and Billy, pick on her. One day Rosie gets so angry with the bullies that she stamps on a crack in the pavement, and two large, furry bears come to her aid. Ben and Billy get a taste of their own medicine, and Rosie finds out she can stand up for herself, and others too.

Bully by David Hughes (Walker, 1995). Girl and Boy are playing with a group of toys and animals. When Dog picks on Teddy 'because he is furry', the bullying begins. Boy sides with the bullies, but Girl and Teddy stick together and face down the bullies.

The Angel of Nitshill Road by Anne Fine (Egmont, 2002). Mysterious Celeste helps her friends deal with the class bully.